Annie & Nico Heesakkers

Embroidery on Paper for Cardmakers

Search Press

Contents

First published in Great Britain 2011 by Search Press Limited, Wellwood, North Farm Road, Tunbridge Wells, Kent TN2 3DR

Reprinted 2012

Original edition published as Borduren op Kaarten by Forte Uitgevers

Copyright © 2005 Forte Uitgevers, Utrecht

English translation by Cicero Translations

English edition produced by GreenGate Publishing Services, Tonbridge

ISBN: 978-1-84448-611-3

Suppliers

If you have any difficulty in obtaining any of the materials and equipment mentioned in this book, please visit the Search Press website for details of suppliers: www.searchpress.com

Although every attempt has been made to ensure that all the materials and equipment used in this book are currently available, the Publishers cannot guarantee that this will always be the case. If you have difficulty in obtaining any of the items mentioned, then suitable alternatives should be used instead.

Printed in Malaysia

Foreword

Dear Embroiderer

You have picked up our first book about embroidery on paper for cardmakers. We've actually done it! Many of you who are familiar with our website have requested a book so we hope that you enjoy it.

We never planned to do this, one of our arguments being that with a book you have to buy a lot of templates when you might only want a few. But when we were asked whether we might be interested in producing a book, we said we'd like to do it and, ultimately, we found it an enjoyable challenge. We wanted everyone who bought this book to say: 'Actually, I like all the templates in it and it is a completely worthwhile purchase.' In addition, with this book we will be able to reach those embroiderers who do not have Internet access.

The book is divided into eight chapters, each with a set of four designs, and every design is graded according to its level of difficulty. The designs are suitable both for beginners and for more advanced embroiderers.

We hope that everyone who buys this book has as much pleasure from the embroidery as we had in creating the designs and putting them together.

You will find hundreds more embroidered examples that we can supply on our website at **www.kaartborduren.nl**

We would like to thank Kars for making the materials available. And thanks also to our daughter-in-law Margreet for her help.

We wish you much pleasure in your embroidery!

Annie & Nico Heesakkers

Embroider your own greetings cards for a personal touch.

Our aim is to create designs for cards that are as pretty as possible. The designs may take any form, from the purely abstract to stars and flowers, etc.

Materials required

- Small sewing needle, size 10 or 11 (do not use an embroidery needle with a blunt tip; these are too thick and will tear the holes in the card)
- Perforating tool
- Pricking mat (felt or heavy foam rubber)
- Small scissors
- Craft knife
- Cutting ruler
- Lacé stencils
- Punches
- Pattern-edged scissors
- cArt-us card
- Lacé Duo card
- Craft pad of shaded paper
- 3D paper
- Pad of Sizzix Little Sizzles Pastels
- Adhesive tape
- Sticky foam tape
- Craft glue
- Small white feathers
- Embroidery thread

We recommend you use Sulky machine embroidery thread. Gutermann, Madeira or DMC threads may also be used. These brands also include metallic threads (with a metallic sheen) and threads with shaded colours, which are also suitable. All these threads can be obtained on reels.

Skeins of DMC thread can be used but these will start unravelling very quickly.

General instructions

1 Attach the card to be embroidered behind the
pricking template with adhesive tape and then
place the two together on the pricking mat
with the pricking template on top.

2 Prick out all the holes through the template
into the card.

3 If you now hold the template up to the light,
you will be able to see whether you have
pricked out all the holes.

4 Detach the card from the template and you can
start embroidering.

Embroidering

Follow the instructions in the examples on the
following page to work the embroidery. When
the instructions refer to threads which run
'across the front', these are the threads that you
can see on the front side of the embroidery. The
threads that remain on the back of the card are
said to run 'behind'. In the instructions it may
say, for example, '1–9' so the thread should
come out at 1 and run across the front to hole 9.
Then it may say '(9–10)' so the thread should be
passed through to the back of the card and run
across the back from 9 to 10.

Note

If you are new to card embroidery, start by
experimenting with the examples on the next page.

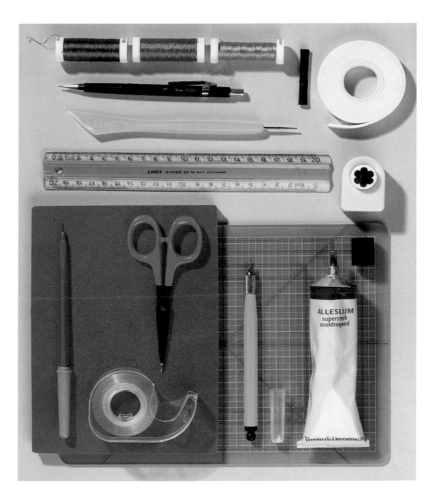

Example 1, angle: from A to B

1 Working from template 1 below, push the needle and thread through from the back to the front at 1 but do not pull the thread right through.

2 Stick about 1cm (⅜in) of thread down on the back of the card with adhesive tape, making sure the tape does not cover the holes.

3 Now pass the thread through at 9, behind to 10, across the front to 2, behind to 3, across the front to 11, etc. The abbreviated instructions for this are as follows:

1–9 (9–10)

10–2 (2–3)

3–11 etc.

Example 2, circle: from X to X

Work the second example in the same way as the first, using template 2 below. The abbreviated instructions for this are as follows:

1–9 (9–10)

10–2 (2–3)

3–11 etc.

At a certain point you will have to use the holes for a second time. Just carry on embroidering until the shape is complete.

Tip

Rub the holes closed with a spatula at the back of the embroidery to obtain an even prettier result.

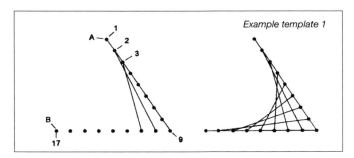

Example template 1

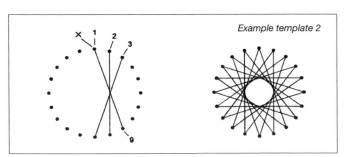

Example template 2

1 Rose-tinted stars

1/1

You will need

- cArt-Us pink card No. 0485: 15 × 21cm (6 × 8in) and 10.5 × 15cm (4 × 6in)
- Paper from a pad of Little Sizzles Pastels in pink
- Sulky embroidery thread 534
- Craft knife and cutting ruler

Instructions

1 First embroider the pattern on the larger card, positioning it as shown in the example on page 7.

2 Using a craft knife and cutting ruler, cut out two triangles of the size shown, positioning them as shown in the example on page 7.

3 Stick the Little Sizzles paper behind the triangular openings.

4 Fold both cards and insert the 10.5 × 15cm (4 × 6in) card.

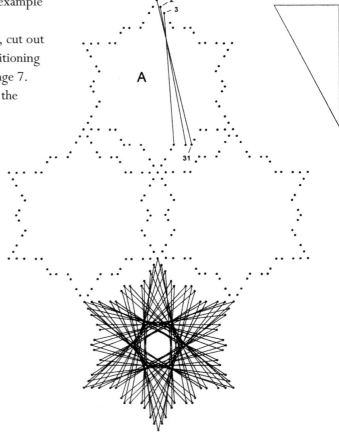

Difficulty level 1

• Figure A

From X to X (4x)

1–31 (31–32)

32–2 (2–3)

3–33 etc.

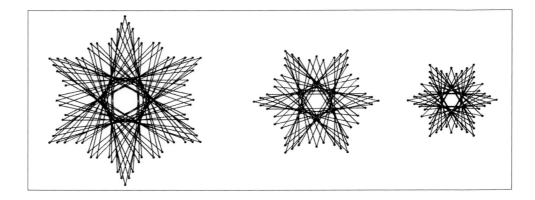

1/2

Instructions

1 First embroider the pattern on the larger card, positioning it as shown in the example on page 7.

2 Fold both cards and insert the 10.5 × 15cm (4 × 6in) card.

3 Cut out the parts of the 3D flowers and use foam tape to stick them in place.

You will need

- cArt-Us pink card No. 0485: 15 × 21cm (6 × 8in) and 10.5 × 15cm (4 × 6in)
- 3D paper 117138/1848, Nel van Veen or other 3D floral motif
- Sulky embroidery threads 534, 1016 and 1017
- Sticky foam tape

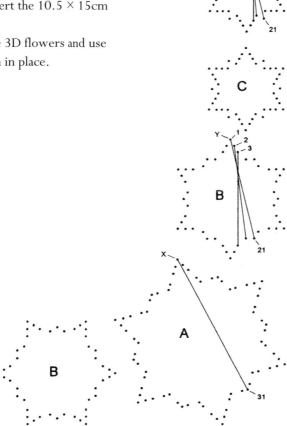

Difficulty level 1

• Figure A

From X to X

1–31 (31–32)

32–2 (2–3)

3–33 etc.

• Figures B and C

From Y to Y

From Z to Z

1–21 (21–22)

22–2 (2–3)

3–23 etc.

1/3

You will need

- cArt-Us pink card No. 0485: 15 × 21cm (6 × 8in) and 10.5 × 15cm (4 × 6in)
- Paper from a pad of Little Sizzles Pastels in pink
- 3D paper 117138/1848 Nel van Veen or other floral 3D motif
- Sulky embroidery threads 534, 1016 and 1017
- Sticky foam tape

Instructions

1 First embroider the pattern on the larger card, positioning it as shown in the example on page 7.
2 Again referring to the finished card, trim off the corners to the desired size.
3 Fold both cards. Stick the Little Sizzles paper to the 10.5 × 15cm (4 × 6in) card first and then insert this behind the embroidery.
4 Cut out the parts of the 3D flower and stick them in place using foam tape.

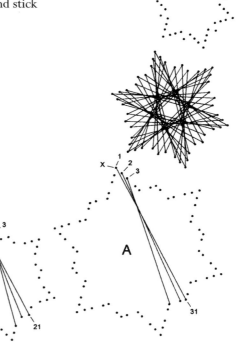

Difficulty level 1

• Figure A
From X to X
1–31 (31–32)
32–2 (2–3)
3–33 etc.
• Figures B and C
From Y to Y
From Z to Z
1–21 (21–22)
22–2 (2–3)
3–23 etc.

Instructions

1 First embroider the pattern on the larger card, positioning it as shown in the example on page 7.

2 Fold both cards and insert the 13.5 × 13.5cm (5¼ × 5¼in) card.

3 Cut out the parts of the 3D flower and use foam tape to stick them in place.

You will need

- cArt-Us pink card No. 0485: 13.5 × 27cm (5¼ × 10½in) and 13.5 × 13.5cm (5¼ × 5¼in)
- 3D paper 117138/1848 Nel van Veen or other floral 3D motif
- Sulky embroidery threads 534, 1016 and 1017
- Sticky foam tape

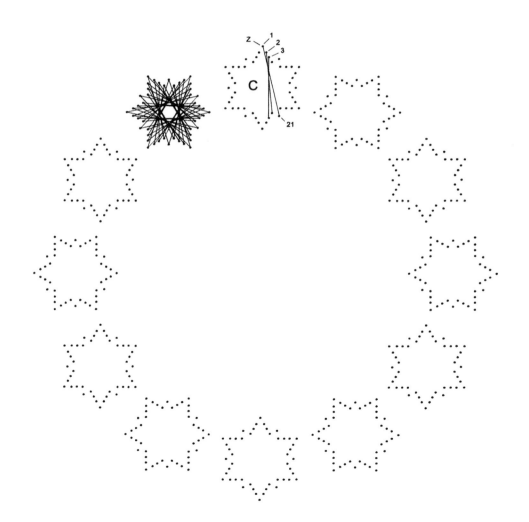

Difficulty level 1

- **Figure C**

From Z to Z

1–21 (21–22)

22–2 (2–3)

3–23 etc.

2 Duo in blue

2/1

You will need

- cArt-Us violet card No. 0487: 15 × 21cm (6 × 8in)
- Lacé Duo card in blue/silver No. 115669–0414: 9.5 × 14cm (3¾ × 5½in)
- Sulky embroidery threads 1239 and 1246
- Lacé stencil 52B

Instructions

1 First embroider the pattern on the Lacé card, placing it centrally.
2 Cut out the points of the top left and bottom-right corners using the Lacé stencil.
3 Fold the cut-out points over so that the silver colour is on top.
4 Fold the violet card and stick the embroidered card centrally on top.

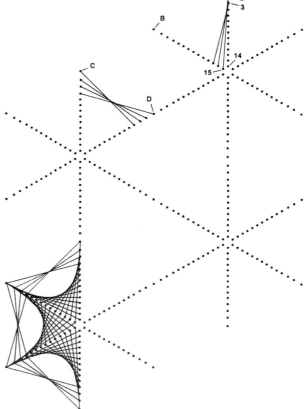

Difficulty level 2

From A to B (24x)

1–15 (15–16)

16–2 (2–3)

3–17 etc.

From C to D (24x)

Embroider as shown in the example.

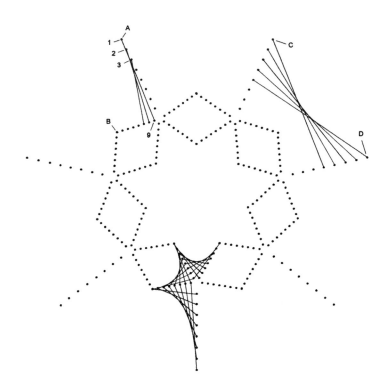

2/2

You will need

- cArt-Us violet card No. 0487: 15 × 21cm (6 × 8in)
- Lacé Duo card in blue/silver No. 115669–0414: 9.5 × 14cm (3¾ × 5½in)
- Sulky embroidery threads 1239 and 1246
- Lacé stencil 52A

Instructions

1 First embroider the pattern on the Lacé card, placing it centrally near the top.
2 Cut out three points from the bottom edge using the Lacé stencil.
3 Turn the stencil over and then cut out the two points between the first three.
4 Fold the cut-out points over so that the silver colour is on top.
5 Fold the violet card and stick the embroidered card centrally on top.

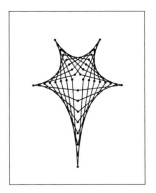

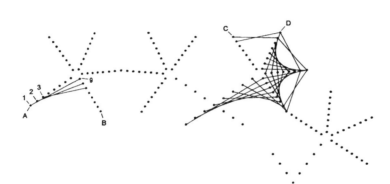

2/3

Instructions

1 First embroider the pattern on the Lacé card, placing it to flow around the top-right corner.

2 Cut out the point in the bottom-left corner using the Lacé stencil.

3 Fold the cut-out point over so that the silver colour is on top.

4 Fold the violet card and stick the embroidered card centrally on top.

5 Cut out the parts of the 3D flowers and use foam tape to stick them in place.

You will need

- cArt-Us violet card No. 0487: 15 × 21cm (6 × 8in)
- Lacé Duo card in blue/silver, No. 115669–0414: 9.5 × 14cm (3¾ × 5½in)
- Sulky embroidery thread 1167
- Lacé stencil 52B
- 3D paper, Shake it 392 or similar floral 3D motif
- Sticky foam tape

Difficulty level 2

From A to B (40x)
1–9 (9–10)
10–2 (2–3)
3–11 etc.
Note The 35 angles of this border have two different shapes but this makes no difference in terms of the embroidery.
From C to D (24x)
Embroider as shown in the example.

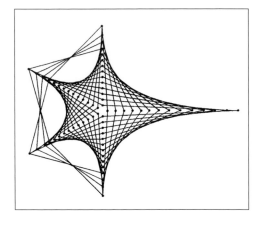

You will need

- cArt-Us violet card No. 0487: 13.5 × 27cm (5¼ × 10½in)
- Lacé Duo card in blue/silver, No. 115669–0414: 12.5 × 12.5cm (5 × 5in)
- Sulky embroidery threads 1167 and 1314

Instructions

1 Embroider the pattern on the Lacé card, placing it centrally.
2 Fold the violet card and stick the embroidered card centrally on top.

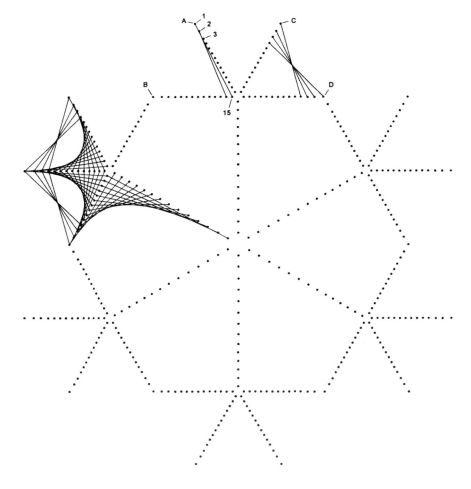

Difficulty level 2

From A to B (30x)

1–15 (15–16)

16–2 (2–3)

3–17 etc.

From C to D (18x)

Embroider as shown in the example.

3 Flowers in pink and green

3/1

Instructions

1 First embroider the pattern on the larger card, positioning it as shown in the example on page 18.

2 Fold both cards and insert the 10.5 × 15cm (4 × 6in) card.

3 Cut out the parts of the 3D flower and use foam tape to stick them in place.

4 Punch the corners using the corner punch.

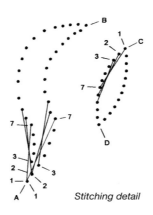

Stitching detail

You will need

- cArt-Us pink card No. 0480: 15 × 21cm (6 × 8in) and 10.5 × 15cm (4 × 6in)
- Sulky embroidery threads 1019 and 1332
- 3D paper 50–245 Le Crea design, Leane de Graaf or similar 3D floral motif
- Rounded corner punch 115635/7001
- Sticky foam tape

Difficulty level 3

From A to B

1–7 (7–8)

8–2 (2–3)

3–9 etc.

From C to D

1–7 (7–8)

8–2 (2–3)

3–9 etc.

Small shapes

Embroider each small shape once on the inner edge and once on the outer edge.

Instructions

1 First embroider the pattern on the larger card, positioning it as shown in the example on page 18.

2 Fold both cards and insert the 10.5 × 15cm (4 × 6in) card.

3 Stick the white feather in the desired position.

4 Cut out the parts of the 3D flowers and use foam tape to stick them on to the white feather.

5 Round off the corners using the corner punch.

You will need

- cArt-Us pink card No. 0480: 15 × 21cm (6 × 8in) and 10.5 × 15cm (4 × 6in)
- Sulky embroidery threads 1019, 1020 and 1332
- 3D paper 117138/1847 Nel van Veen or similar 3D floral motif
- Rounded corner punch 115635/7001
- White feather
- Sticky foam tape

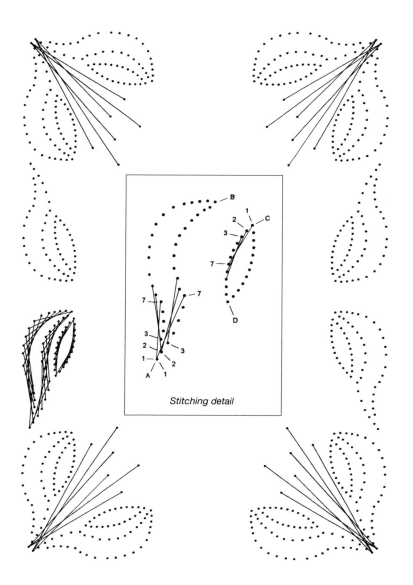

Stitching detail

Difficulty level 3

From A to B
1–7 (7–8)
8–2 (2–3)
3–9 etc.

From C to D
1–7 (7–8)
8–2 (2–3)
3–9 etc.

Small shapes
Embroider each small shape once on the inner edge and once on the outer edge.

Stamens
Embroider as shown in the example.

3/3

You will need

- cArt-Us pink card No. 0480: 15 × 21cm (6 × 8in)
- Strip of cArt-Us pink card No. 0481: 4.5 × 20cm (1¾ × 8in)
- Sulky embroidery threads 1019 and 1332
- 3D paper 50–245 Le Crea design, Leane de Graaf or similar 3D floral motif
- Pattern-edged scissors 118500/0703
- Rounded corner punch 115635/7001
- Three small white feathers
- Sticky foam tape

Difficulty level 3

From A to B

1–7 (7–8)

8–2 (2–3)

3–9 etc.

From C to D

1–7 (7–8)

8–2 (2–3)

3–9 etc.

Small shapes

Embroider each small shape once on the inner edge and once on the outer edge.

Stamens

Embroider as shown in the example.

Instructions

1 First embroider the pattern along the centre of the card strip.

2 Use the pattern-edged scissors to trim both long edges of the embroidered strip.

3 Fold the card and stick the embroidered strip diagonally on to the front; trim off any surplus.

4 Stick the three small white feathers in the desired position.

5 Cut out the parts of the 3D flower and use foam tape to stick them on to the feathers.

6 Round off the corners using the corner punch.

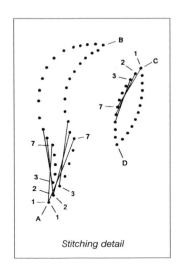

Stitching detail

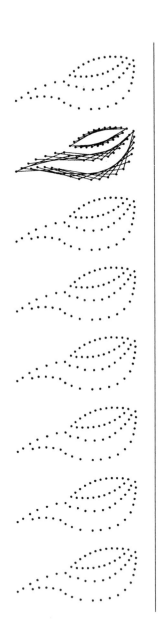

3/4

Instructions

1 First embroider the pattern on the larger card, positioning it as shown in the example on page 18.
2 Fold both cards and insert the 13.5 × 13.5cm (5¼ × 5¼in) card.
3 Cut out the parts of the 3D flower and use foam tape to stick them in place.
4 Round off the corners using the corner punch.

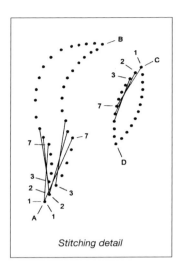

Stitching detail

You will need

- cArt-Us pink card No. 0480: 13.5 × 27cm (5¼ × 10½in) and 13.5 × 13.5cm (5¼ × 5¼in)
- Sulky embroidery threads 1019, 1020 and 1332
- 3D paper 117138/1849 Nel van Veen or similar 3D floral motif
- Rounded corner punch 115635/7001
- Sticky foam tape

Difficulty level 3

From A to B
1–7 (7–8)
8–2 (2–3)
3–9 etc.

From C to D
1–7 (7–8)
8–2 (2–3)
3–9 etc.

Small shapes
Embroider each small shape once on the inner edge and once on the outer edge.

Stamens
Embroider as shown in the example.

4 Blue waves

4/1

You will need

- cArt-Us blue card No. 0427: 15 × 21cm (6 × 8in)
- cArt-Us cream card No. 0241: 9.5 × 14cm (3¾ × 5½in)
- Scraps of card in mid and light blue and in mid and light green
- Sulky embroidery threads 572 and 1095
- Flower and leaf punches 115635/0084, 115635/0085, 115635/0086, 115635/8071 and 115635/0065
- Sticky foam tape

Instructions

1 First embroider the pattern on the cream card, positioning it as shown in the example on page 23.
2 Fold the blue card and stick the embroidered card centrally on top.
3 Punch out small flowers and leaves from blue and green card and use foam tape to stick these in place.

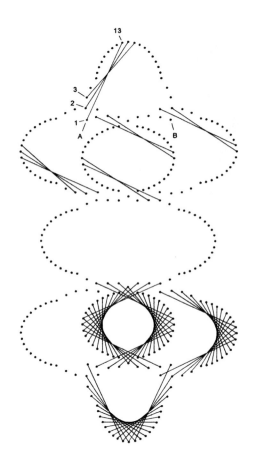

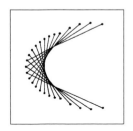

Difficulty level 3

From A to B (12x)

1–13 (13–14)

14–2 (2–3)

3–15 etc.

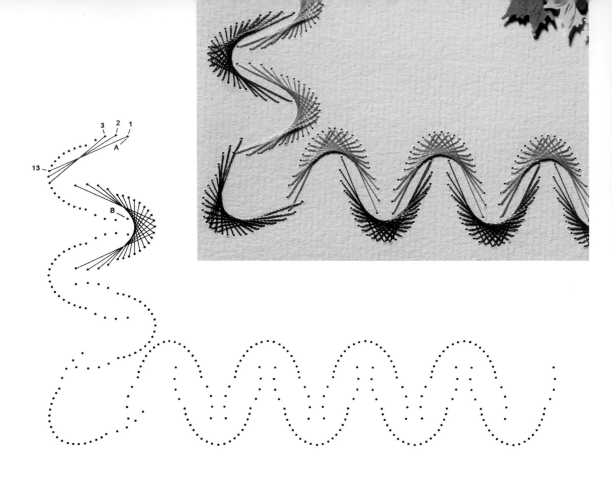

4/2

You will need

- cArt-Us blue card No. 0427: 15 × 21cm (6 × 8in)
- cArt-Us cream card No. 0241: 9.5 × 14cm (3¾ × 5½in)
- Scraps of card in dark and mid blue and in pale and mid green
- Sulky embroidery threads 1095 and 1096
- Flower and leaf punches 115635/8067, 115635/8071, 115635/0058, 115635/0065 and 115635/0067
- Sticky foam tape

Difficulty level 1

From A to B (13x)

1–13 (13–14)

14–2 (2–3)

3–15 etc.

Instructions

1 First embroider the pattern on the cream card, positioning it as shown in the example on page 23.

2 Fold the blue card and stick the embroidered card centrally on top.

3 Punch out the small flowers and leaves and use foam tape to stick these in place.

4/3

Instructions

1 First embroider the pattern on the blue strip with the curves of the shape 4mm (⅛in) from the edge. Cut waves along the lines of the shape.

2 Stick the strip diagonally on to the cream card and trim off any surplus.

3 Fold the blue card and stick the decorated card centrally on top.

4 Punch out the small flowers and leaves and use foam tape to stick these in place.

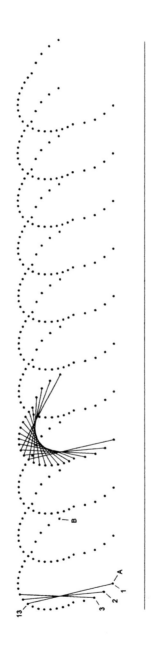

You will need

- cArt-Us blue card No. 0427: 15 × 21cm (6 × 8in)
- cArt-Us cream card No. 0241: 9.5 × 14cm (3¾ × 5½in)
- Strip of cArt-Us blue card No. 0391: 4.5 × 20cm (1¾ × 8in)
- Scraps of card in light and mid blue and in pale and mid green
- Sulky embroidery thread 1076
- Flower and leaf punches 115635/0080, 115635/8058, 115635/0084, 115635/8071 and 115635/0058
- Sticky foam tape

Difficulty level 3

From A to B (11x)

1–13 (13–14)

14–2 (2–3)

3–15 etc.

You will need

- cArt-Us blue card No. 0427: 13.5 × 27cm (5¼ × 10½in)
- cArt-Us cream card No. 0241: 12.5 × 12.5cm (5 × 5in)
- Sulky embroidery threads 572 and 1095

Instructions

1 Embroider the pattern, placing it centrally on the cream card.

2 Fold the blue card and stick the embroidered card centrally on top.

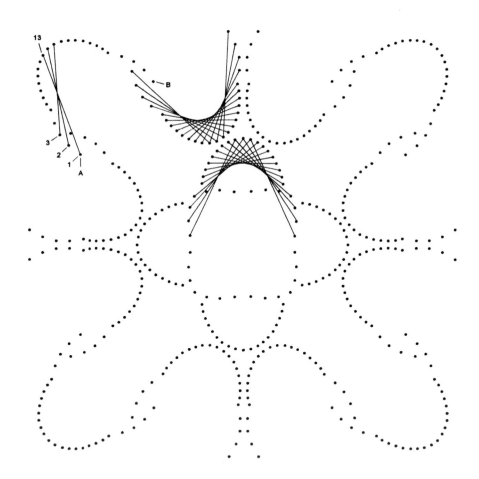

Difficulty level 4

From A to B (16x)

1–13 (13–14)

14–2 (2–3)

3–15 etc.

5 Greens entwined

5/1

Instructions

1 First embroider the pattern on the pale green card, placing it just above the centre.

2 Fold the mid green card and stick the embroidered card centrally on top.

3 Cut out the parts of the 3D flowers and use foam tape to stick them in place in the lower-left corner.

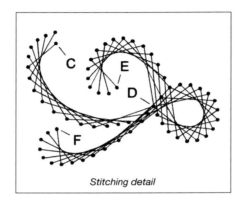

Stitching detail

You will need

- cArt-Us mid green card No. 0367: 15 × 21cm (6 × 8in)
- cArt-Us pale green card No. 0331: 9.5 × 14cm (3¾ × 5½in)
- Sulky embroidery threads 1051, 1156 and 1209
- 3D paper 117145/1018 Picturel or similar 3D floral motif
- Sticky foam tape

Difficulty level 4

From A to B

1–11 (11–12)

12–2 (2–3)

3–13 etc.

From C to D

1–7 (7–8)

8–2 (2–3)

3–9 etc.

From E to F

1–7 (7–8)

8–2 (2–3)

3–9 etc.

5/2

Instructions

1 First embroider the pattern centrally on the pale green card.

2 Fold the mid green card and stick the embroidered card centrally on top.

3 Cut out the parts of the 3D flowers and use foam tape to stick them in place in the centre of the design.

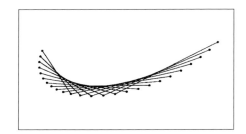

You will need

- cArt-Us mid green card No. 0367: 15 × 21cm (6 × 8in)
- cArt-Us pale green card No. 0331: 9.5 × 14cm (3¾ × 5½in)
- Sulky embroidery threads 1156, 1209 and 1245
- 3D paper, 117145/1018 Picturel or similar 3D floral motif
- Sticky foam tape

Difficulty level 4

From A to B

1–11 (11–12)

12–2 (2–3)

3–13 etc.

From C to D

1–7 (7–8)

8–2 (2–3)

3–9 etc.

From E to F

1–7 (7–8)

8–2 (2–3)

3–9 etc.

5/3

You will need

- cArt-Us mid green card No. 0367: 15 × 21cm (6 × 8in)
- cArt-Us pale green card No. 0331: 9.5 × 14cm (3¾ × 5½in)
- Sulky embroidery threads 1156 and 1209
- 3D paper Picturel 117145/1018 or similar 3D floral motif
- Sticky foam tape

Instructions

1 First embroider the pattern on the pale green card, placing it deliberately off-centre to allow room for the 3D flowers.
2 Fold the mid green card and stick the embroidered card centrally on top.
3 Cut out the parts of the 3D flowers and use foam tape to stick them in place.

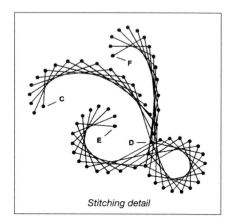

Stitching detail

Difficulty level 4

From C to D

1–7 (7–8)

8–2 (2–3)

3–9 etc.

From E to F

1–7 (7–8)

8–2 (2–3)

3–9 etc.

5/4

Instructions

1 Embroider the pattern centrally on the pale green card.
2 Fold the mid green card and stick the embroidered card centrally on top.

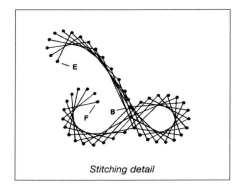

Stitching detail

You will need

- cArt-Us mid green card No. 0367: 13.5 × 27cm (5¼ × 10½in)
- cArt-Us pale green card No. 0331: 12.5 × 12.5cm (5 × 5in)
- Sulky embroidery threads 1051, 1049 and 1245

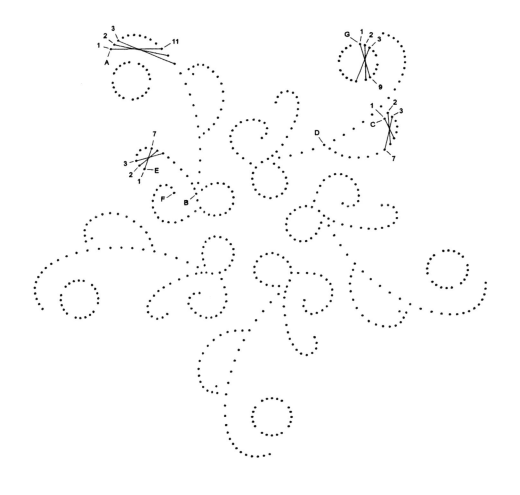

Difficulty level 4

From A to B (5x)
1–11 (11–12)
12–2 (2–3)
3–13 etc.

From C to D (5x)
1–7 (7–8)
8–2 (2–3)
3–9 etc.

From E to F (5x)
1–7 (7–8)
8–2 (2–3)
3–9 etc.

From G to G (5x)
1–9 (9–10)
10–2 (2–3)
3–11 etc.

6
Violet and purple frames

6/1

Instructions

1 Embroider the pattern on the larger card, positioning it as shown in the example on page 32.
2 Fold both cards and insert the 10.5 × 15cm (4 × 6in) card.

You will need

- cArt-Us yellow card No. 0275: 15 × 21cm (6 × 8in) and 10.5 × 15cm (4 × 6in)
- Sulky embroidery threads 1033 and 1195

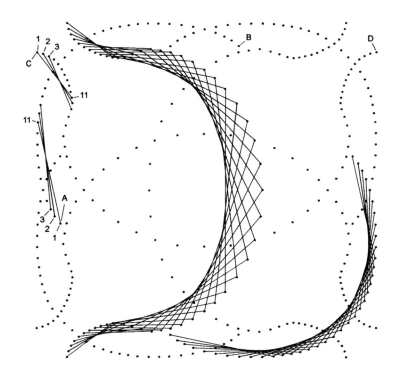

Difficulty level 4

From A to B (4x)
1–11 (11–12)
12–2 (2–3)
3–13 etc.
From C to D (4x)
1–11 (11–12)
12–2 (2–3)
3–13 etc.

6/2

You will need

- cArt-Us yellow card No. 0275: 15 × 21cm (6 × 8in) and 10.5 × 15cm (4 × 6in)
- Sulky embroidery threads 1033 and 1195
- 3D paper Picturel 117145/1018 or similar 3D floral motif
- Sticky foam tape

Instructions

1 First embroider the pattern on the larger card, positioning it as shown in the example on page 32.

2 Fold both cards and insert the 10.5 × 15cm (4 × 6in) card.

3 Cut out the parts of the 3D flower and use foam tape to stick them in place.

Difficulty level 3

From A to B (8x)

1–11 (11–12)

12–2 (2–3)

3–13 etc.

From C to D (8x)

1–11 (11–12)

12–2 (2–3)

3–13 etc.

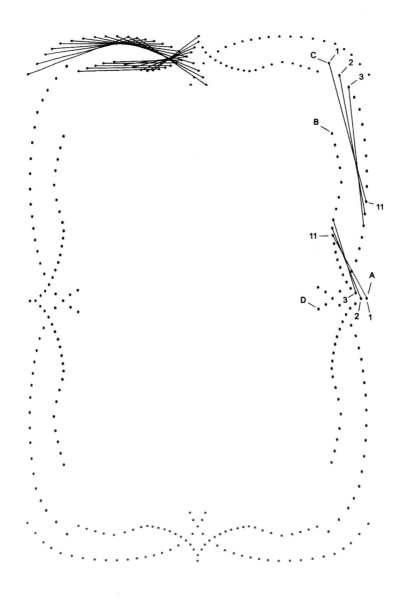

6/3

Instructions

1 First embroider the pattern, positioning it as shown in the example on page 32.
2 Fold both cards and insert the 10.5 × 15cm (4 × 6in) card.
3 Cut out a small flower and use foam tape to stick this in place.

You will need

- cArt-Us yellow card No. 0275: 15 × 21cm (6 × 8in) and 10.5 × 15cm (4 × 6in)
- Sulky embroidery threads 1193 and 1195
- 3D paper 117138/1849 Nel van Veen or similar 3D floral motif
- Sticky foam tape

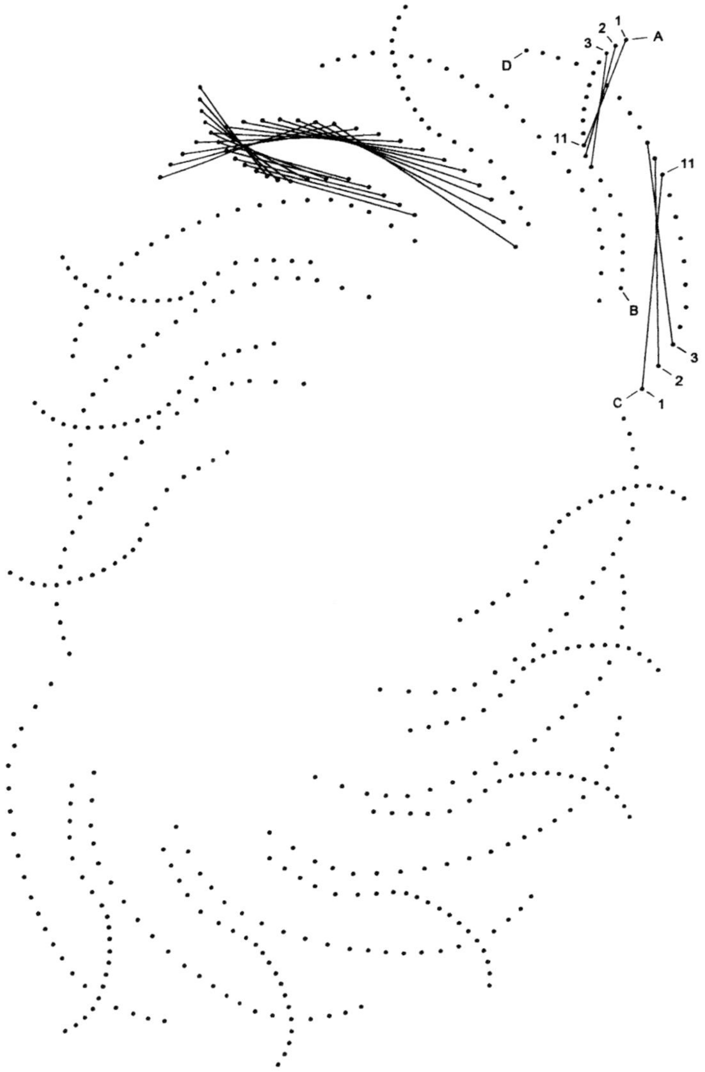

Difficulty level 2

From A to B (12x)

1–11 (11–12)

12–2 (2–3)

3–13 etc.

From C to D (12x)

1–11 (11–12)

12–2 (2–3)

3–13 etc.

6/4

You will need

- cArt-Us yellow card No. 0275: 13.5 × 27cm (5¼ × 10½in) and 13.5 × 13.5cm (5¼ × 5¼in)
- Sulky embroidery threads 1033 and 1276
- 3D paper 117138/1849 Nel van Veen or similar 3D floral motif
- Sticky foam tape

Instructions

1 First embroider the pattern on the larger card, positioning it as shown in the example on page 32.

2 Fold both cards and insert the 13.5 × 13.5cm (5¼ × 5¼in) card.

3 Cut out the parts of the 3D flower and use foam tape to stick them in place.

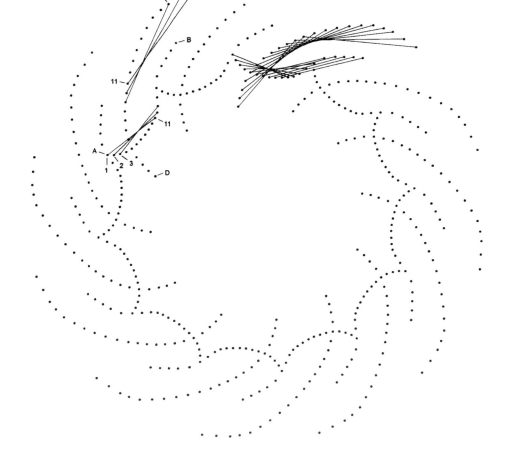

Difficulty level 3

From A to B (12x)

1–11 (11–12)

12–2 (2–3)

3–13 etc.

From C to D (12x)

1–11 (11–12)

12–2 (2–3)

3–13 etc.

7
Energising blue

7/1

Instructions

1 Embroider the pattern centrally on the Lacé card.
2 Fold the blue card and stick the embroidered card centrally on top.

You will need

- cArt-Us royal blue card No. 0417: 15 × 21cm (6 × 8in)
- Lacé Duo card No. 115669/0402: 9.5 × 14cm (3¾ × 5½in)
- Sulky embroidery threads 561, 1017 and 1185

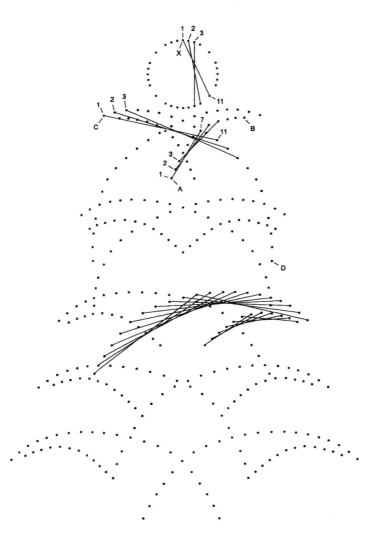

Difficulty level 3

From A to B (10x)
1–7 (7–8)
8–2 (2–3)
3–9 etc.

From C to D (10x)
1–11 (11–12)
12–2 (2–3)
3–13 etc.

From X to X
1–11 (11–12)
12–2 (2–3)
3–13 etc.

7/2

Instructions

1 First embroider the pattern centrally on the Lacé card.
2 Fold the blue card and stick the embroidered card centrally on top.
3 Cut out the parts of the 3D flowers and use foam tape to stick them in place at the centre of the embroidery.

You will need

- cArt-Us royal blue card No. 0417: 15 × 21cm (6 × 8in)
- Lacé Duo card No. 115669/0402: 9.5 × 14cm (3¾ × 5½in)
- Sulky embroidery threads 1017 and 1065
- 3D paper Picturel No. 117145/1018 or similar 3D floral motif
- Sticky foam tape

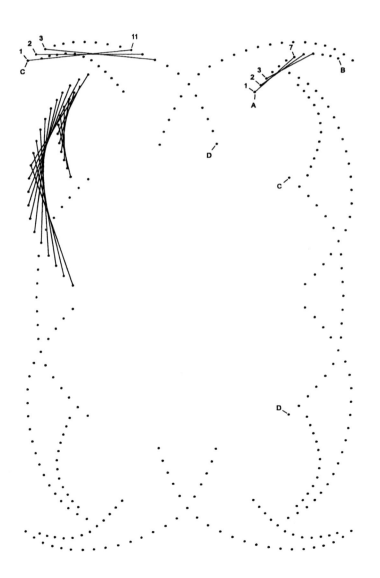

Difficulty level 3

From A to B (8x)

1–7 (7–8)

8–2 (2–3)

3–9 etc.

From C to D (10x)

1–11 (11–12)

12–2 (2–3)

3–13 etc.

7/3

You will need

- cArt-Us royal blue card No. 0417: 15 × 21cm (6 × 8in)
- Lacé Duo card No. 115669/0402: 9.5 × 14cm (3¾ × 5½in)
- Sulky embroidery threads 572, 1017 and 1185
- Lacé stencil No. 42

Instructions

1 First embroider the pattern centrally on the Lacé card.
2 Cut off two corners 2 × 2cm (¾ × ¾in), as shown in the example on page 38.
3 Now cut out the ellipses using the Lacé stencil. Fold the cut-out curves over so that the white colour is at the top.
4 Fold the blue card and stick the embroidered card centrally on top.

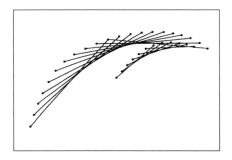

Difficulty level 2

From A to B (8x)

1–7 (7–8)

8–2 (2–3)

3–9 etc.

From C to D (8x)

1–11 (11–12)

12–2 (2–3)

3–13 etc.

From X to X

1–7 (7–8)

8–2 (2–3)

3–9 etc.

Note Use all the holes twice.

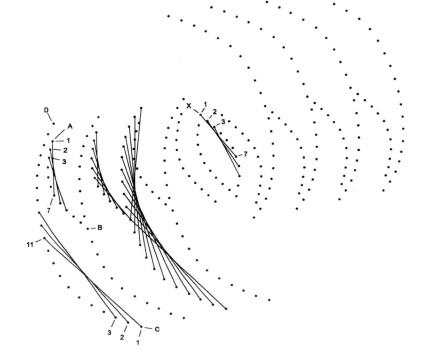

7/4

Instructions

1 First embroider the pattern on the Lacé card, placing it towards the top-left corner.
2 Cut off a corner 2 × 2cm (¾ × ¾in), as shown in the example on page 38.
3 Starting at the trimmed corner, cut out the five ellipses using the Lacé stencil. Fold the cut-out curves over so that the white colour is at the top.
4 Fold the blue card and stick the embroidered card centrally on top.

You will need

- cArt-Us royal blue card No. 0417: 13.5 × 27cm (5¼ × 10½in)
- Lacé Duo card No. 115669/0402: 12.5 × 12.5cm (5 × 5in)
- Sulky embroidery threads 561, 572, 1017 and 1065
- Lacé stencil No. 42

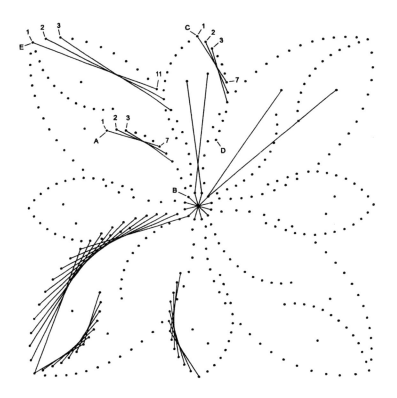

Difficulty level 4

From A to B (8x)

1–7 (7–8)

8–2 (2–3)

3–9 etc.

From C to D (8x)

1–7 (7–8)

8–2 (2–3)

3–9 etc.

From E to B (8x)

1–11 (11–12)

12–2 (2–3)

3–13 etc.

Note Embroider the remaining lines as shown in the example.

8 Floral compositions

Method for all templates

Instructions

Because these are very full pricking templates, we prick out the cards in two stages. This makes it considerably easier to embroider the patterns.

1 Start by pricking out the points on the template that are connected to one another by the lines.
2 Embroider the frames in black thread and all the other lines in green.
3 Place the pricking template back on the card and use the corners of the frame to centre the template. Use four pins to fix the template and the card firmly to the pricking mat. Prick out all the remaining points.
4 Complete the embroidery.
5 Fold the cards and insert the smaller card to cover the back of the embroidery.

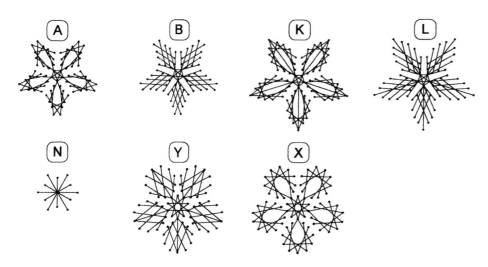

8/1

You will need

- Orange Hobby card No. 115511/0003: 15 × 21cm (6 × 8in) and 10.5 × 15cm (4 × 6in)
- Sulky embroidery threads 561, 572, 1005, 1023, 1033, 1051 and 1252

Instructions

1 Read through the instructions on page 43 before you begin. Working on the larger card, embroider the frame and vase in black and the stems and leaves in green, as instructed.

2 Embroider the flowers as shown in the examples on page 43, using the corresponding letter in each case.

3 Fold both cards and insert the 10.5 × 15cm (4 × 6in) card.

Difficulty level 5

Vase

From C to D (2x)

1–7 (7–8)

8–2 (2–3)

3–9 etc.

From E to F

1–7 (7–8)

8–2 (2–3)

3–9 etc.

Embroider the remaining lines of the vase as shown in the example.

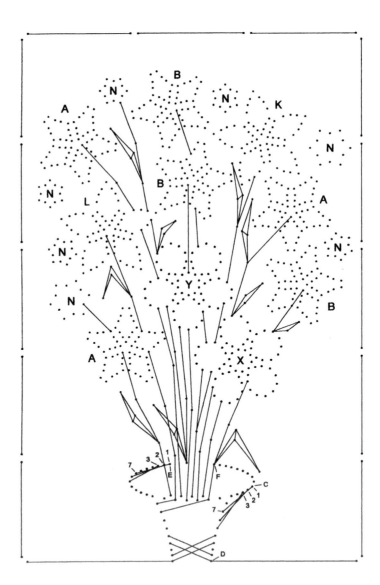

8/2

Instructions

1 Read through the instructions on page 43 before you begin. Working on the larger card, embroider the frame in black and the stems and leaves in green, as instructed.

2 Embroider the flowers as shown in the examples on page 43, using the corresponding letter in each case.

3 Fold both cards and insert the 10.5 × 15cm (4 × 6in) card.

You will need

- Orange Hobby card No. 115511/0003: 15 × 21cm (6 × 8in) and 10.5 × 15cm (4 × 6in)
- Sulky embroidery threads 561, 572, 1005, 1023, 1033, 1051 and 1252

Difficulty level 5

8/3

You will need

- Orange Hobby card No. 115511/0003: 15 × 21cm (6 × 8in) and 10.5 × 15cm (4 × 6in)
- Sulky embroidery threads 561, 572, 1005, 1051 and 1252

Instructions

1 Read through the instructions on page 43 before you begin. Working on the larger card, embroider the frame in black and the leaves in green, as instructed.

2 Embroider the flowers as shown in the examples on page 43, using the corresponding letter in each case.

3 Fold both cards and insert the 10.5 × 15cm (4 × 6in) card.

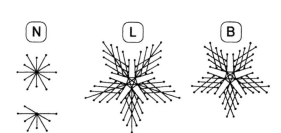

Difficulty level 5

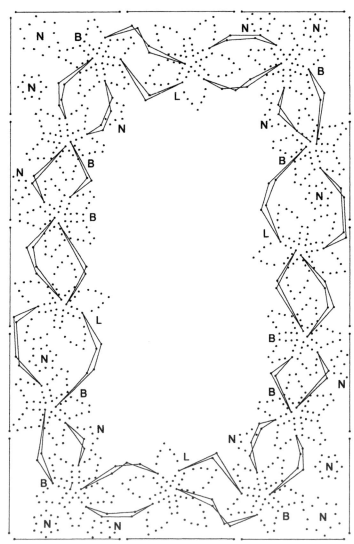

8/4

Instructions

1 Read through the instructions on page 43 before you begin. Working on the orange card, embroider the frame in black and the leaves in green, as instructed.

2 Embroider the flowers as shown in the examples on page 43, using the corresponding letter in each case.

3 Fold the white card and stick the embroidered card centrally on top.

You will need

- cArt-Us white card No. 0210: 13.5 × 27cm (5¼ × 10½in)
- Orange Hobby card No. 115511/0003: 13.5 × 13.5cm (5¼ × 5¼in)
- Sulky embroidery threads 561, 572, 1005, 1023, 1033, 1051 and 1252

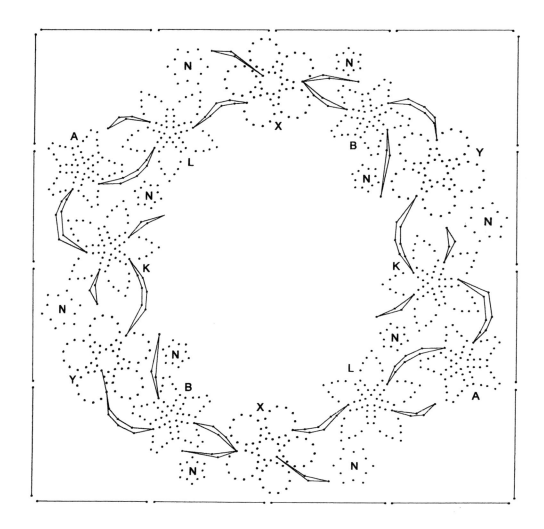

Difficulty level 5